I0212797

brackish

poems by

nicole bethune winters

Finishing Line Press
Georgetown, Kentucky

brackish

Publisher: Leah Huete de Maines
Editor: Christen Kincaid
Cover Art: Colton Zobel
Author Photo: Colton Zobel
Cover Design: Elizabeth Maines McCleavy

Order online: www.finishinglinepress.com
         also available on amazon.com

Author inquiries and mail orders:
Finishing Line Press
P. O. Box 1626
Georgetown, Kentucky 40324
U. S. A.

table of contents

to the ones born from the ocean

"*I cannot fix on the hour, or the spot, or the look or the words, which laid the foundation. it is too long ago. I was in the middle before I knew that I had begun.*"

—*jane austen, pride and prejudice*

moon

ocean gorged, engulfing—

one october
at witching hour,
the waxing gibbous
crossed through pisces
& two weeks early,
I leapt from my mother's
womb.

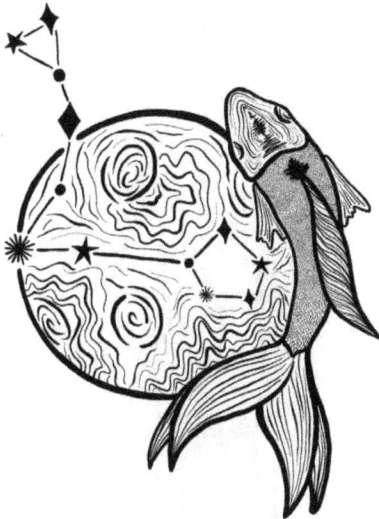

learning to swim

coins glint silver & bronze
in the   deep end—
dive

         down
         entwined legs
a tail   &   fins.

try to pick up ten
in one breath,
& emerge   choking
on chlorine

the first time

teasing waves—
feet tickled by foam

til' water
       swallowed castles
            at high tide.

arms spread, wings
            flapping wild

held warm by ginger
painted sky, footsteps
            heavy with sleep
            left scars
washed away by salt.

nightmare

screams & sweat wake,
a ship—billowing
sails pierce midnight clouds;

rogue waves splinter wooden
hull, & full moon
floods the deck,

lightning strikes the mast,
screaming sail tears, and

my father jumps the rail
to thrashing swells.

deployment

I have to use a stepstool
to see the countries at the top;
trace a finger over   topography—
feel mountain ranges
and ocean trenches.
color-coated thumbtacks

where my father is,   lost
in open ocean
or foreign shore-
bound. every time he moves,

momma hands me a tack &
together   we press it
into the drywall.

evolutions

i.
when I was three, I teased
crashing waves, determined
to outrun foam.

ii.
at ten,
I closed my eyes & sprinted
through shore break;
                    trusting
sandbar to break my fall.

iii.
when I turned fourteen
saltwater sprung
sanguine & seaweed
flourished; waves volatile.

iv.
at eighteen, I bathed
topless   in the salt, floating
hair wild; skin scathed
                    by shells.

v.
but, after twenty-five evolutions
around the sun, brine
became oxygen

I dive
          straight into the foam;

& carve my journey
in wet earth.

chasing the sunrise

sliver of sienna glow shines
          through indigo, smothered
          in pastel cumulus. leaning
into sand, barebacked as ocean laps
              against shore,

listen to the conch. peach
oyster shells match sun-stained sky.

a sharp light stretches arms
across horizon.
          closer to the water the sun rises—

I dive;
buried in light.

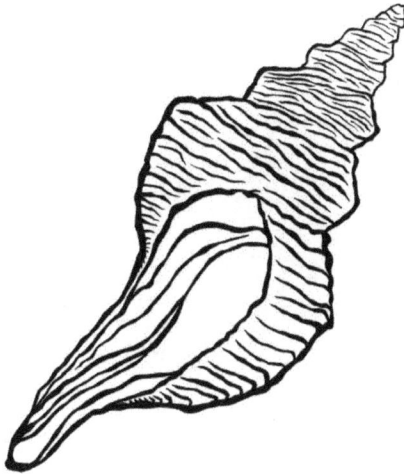

homecoming

rouged shoulders
match the rubies my father
found in afghanistan.
anemic & blush, set
one in silver around
middle finger as
he returns with the sun.

5:32am

humidity fogs the windshield
& as amethyst sky gleams
sweat drops
       & pothole splashes
burn chapped lips.

hair spills into wind
singing to sand-lined asphalt.

wind whispers tides
& in the cul-de-sac
behind the church on 15th,
waves crash beneath my feet.

home

in the salt
encrusted pilings.
water recesses &
I'm anchored to

a piece of me buried
between sea & sand;

it pulls the moon.

burnt

sunbursts ignite fires,
mirror flames reaching
through cosmos, blistering

from the inside out.
secrets and spirit broil
between equinoxes

in underglaze brushed
over greenware flesh
marred with sgraffito

so the scars shine white
against tanned skin.

raptor

stroking just beyond the break,
gliding through fish squirming
against stomach,

an osprey hovers;
white-bellied, mottled
sun-tanned freckles.

she folds her wings
in free fall—plummeting
talons deploy,
break through glass.

diving behind her,
time ceases,
            oxygen drains;

vision blurs in salt
& sand is swirled to bloodied
silt.

muted struggles churn
foam beneath breakers
and then   stillness.

we gasp
at the same time,
            spit salt from beak,

treading together
til' wings pull
            her from whitewater,
a flounder limp
pierced in her grasp.

birth moon

born under a waxing gibbous,

carving flesh from clay
like saline burrowing stone
laying trails in sand

like the sleep rubbed
away at sunrise   exfoliating
          the skin under eyes

that glimpse the future
in forgotten wave foam
& coffee grounds
arranged neat in cobalt.

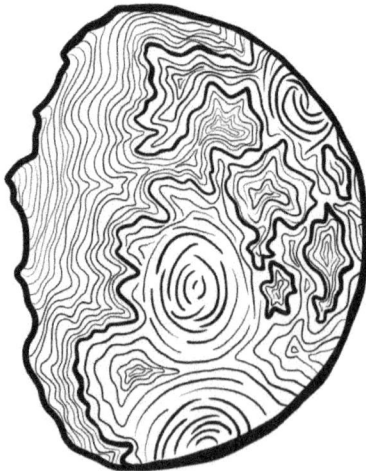

water sign

the sun casts gold
　　　　on the moon & I found
a piece of my soul
in indigo.

beach kids

collect oyster shells
at low tide   weave
through honeysuckle growing
along narrows   wrapped
around the trunks of trees
since the cavalier lawn
stretched to sand—

the sunrise is best by the pier,
climb weathered stands
exposed nails rusted
with names carved
through peeling paint,

buy handmade jewelry
from the crystal lady on saturday
& run on sundays at 8am
through trails canopied
in spanish moss

& sneak into sand
dunes hidden
in seagrass valleys
watching the ospreys' skydance.

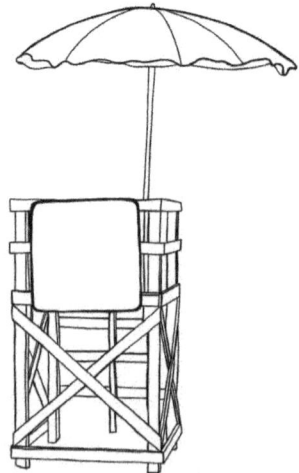

sienna

skin sunburnt at golden hour;

amber glass shards,
a bottle of vanilla extract,
salt-corroded light

dancing on the tree
canopy whispering

to fresh rain saturated
clay between toes
or tree flesh exposed
behind peeling bark
sloughing

salt-soaked sandalwood basking,
the skin of a conch
or gentle burn of incense.

some days fresh
from that broken bottle—
teeth bared, slicing;

but mostly wave beaten,
frosted edges softened
        low tide at dawn
and the final breath
of smoke.

everywhere

i.
the important pages are earmarked,
worn thin with fingered edges,
I remember the words
that make me fall

       in love, and even more,
the ones that hurt;

throw my book against the wall,
watch it smack
and slide;
           it never falls quickly.
I pick it up because
I need to know
what happens.

ii.
salt sticks to the pages of books,
it plagues the air and folds into sand,
saturates the ocean and floats seaweed

to the surface. salt sticks to my hair, too,
fingers it as the wind blows,
brushing loose strands from my

cheek. I brush salt from my skin
after the sun evaporates sweat, and think

the sun is my lover, warming
from the inside out.

iii.
salt and sand follow
       me everywhere, hide
in my bedsheets, get stuck in wrinkles
from feet thrashing

sometimes,

I remember to shower; hot water
      reminds me of the sun, the
drops like palms running
down my spine
      and legs.

petrichor

walk in the woods after rainfall,
   tree leaves drip
   fresh pools
into slick clay
rooted together &

the air tastes of pine, cedarwood
& honeysuckle; clouds tamper sun
   painting leaves lime & jade.

dig your toes in the warm silt
& the trees will whisper secrets
to fill your lungs.

process

over the stoneware
breath synchronizes
with the rhythm of mud
trapped oxygen.

at the end, I slice
to see if any pockets survived,
but it's just earth.

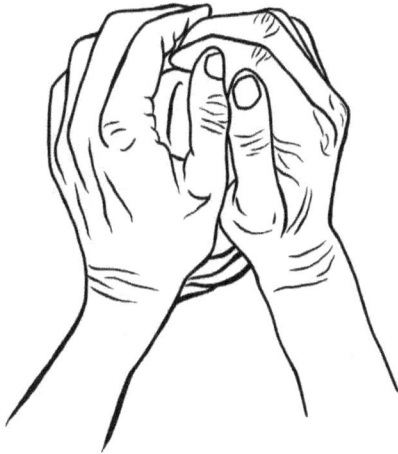

rappahannock

an osprey drowns ceaseless
crickets and cicadas.

rocks churn the river;
rapids roil speckled
with algae & shoots of water grass.

a lull of stillness:
        resonate glass
        marred with silt.

running alongside hickory shad
racing from salt to spawn,

the indigo light of dusk
washes my lungs.

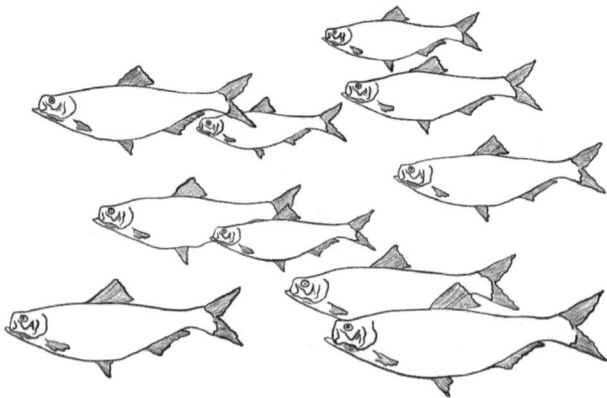

we live on the same time;

the sun rises earliest over the ocean;
the beat of waves clicks
seconds where we met;

set my new sports watch. ticks
digital numbers so they match
                              and blink
a matching turquoise at 6am.

the sun rises three minutes earlier over the bay
than it does over the river;

a breeze pushes the sundial;
our clocks keep ticking swells.

de longhi

on my twenty-first birthday
dad sent an espresso machine—
so instead of tequila chased with lime
it was bold hyperion blend,
ground fine as salt;

tamp,
        just the right pressure,

& boiling water extracts
in three parts:

sienna foam
that lures with honeyed
tease of cocoa

caramel like terra cotta
if pulled right,

and the bitter chaser
that lingers.

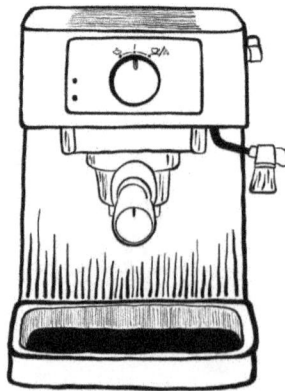

how to properly brew an undertow:

pull one shot of espresso
on a base of two pumps of vanilla syrup,
& pour one inch of cold milk
over the back of a spoon,
& there's a shot of ocean,
just missing the salt.

swells

foam crashes, catching stomach;
lean into it, cascade down

salt ripples away from fins
and time changes in moving water
flying down the side of a wave

rearing back; foam lunges
at its peak and curls.
fingers comb glass and
wind whispers through wet hair
as indigo churns brown;
a slow sweep—

tumult, scrape against sandbar
until the last stretch

leaves my lungs;
when my head breaks
through, breath collides,
restarts the clock.

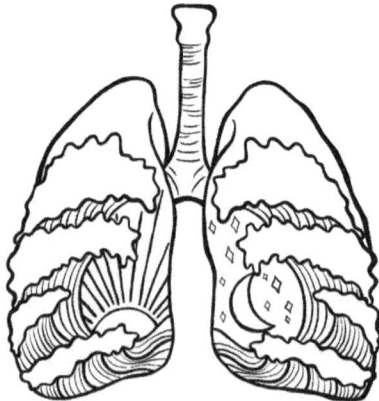

the practice

palms open, chanting
with the hum of morning
doves' coo

a wick of palo santo crackles
into sage-cleansed breath
and my blood pulsates to tides waxing
with my birth moon.

super-moon meditation

women sitting
                     in meditation
 smile, and flip
their palms toward the sky.

the moon is rising,
           crawling up the skyline
towards the shadow   of the sun. energy
radiates
          down to earth,
the tides   rise, and
the ocean   roughens.

 a single sliver   blinks red,
grows,   silver light
                             shrinks.
as blood thaws

the sun illuminates
                   red wine;
warmth trickles
          down
to patient palms.

breath mimics the pull of tides
       in   and   out
through the body;
lotus flowers bloom
                 from the sit-bones

now, the moon's power   wanes;
          blood refreezes.
the ocean calms,

palms flip
          to face the ground;

sticks of incense   sigh
final tails of smoke.

reflection

compress stoneware to wheel,
& add water
   the bat spins.
pressing down,

two fingers open center
pull walls,
create a cavern—

there's no grog &
clay glides against palm heel

grow hips like venus,
smooth the rim
watch her twirl
     round'
sponge slip, & cut her off
her pedestal.

flight patterns

sun glistens off skyscrapers & squeezes
blackout curtains, brushing
                eggshell sheets.

stoplights blink rush hour
         rhythms, neon signs buzz
open, bagel bakeries waft
             soft dough down
             alleyways,
a pigeon takes flight at dawn.

bundled in burgundy,
breath soft with sleep—
eyes flutter,

hiding in beige dunes,
             grazing seagrass
             with salted skin
listening to gulls squawking
at sand crabs sprinting for their tunnels
wrapped together
like snarled seaweed—

eyes open like the ocean
& I stretch my wings

curl together
             ready to nest.

midsummer

indigo sky wakes;
gold luster lines
        horizon by the pier
sage glazed incense tray
faces the receding tide. pull

a stick of sandalwood
& press it into the center, strike a match
whisper flame to sienna glow,

smoke diffuses into salt & hum.

skin prickles as sun
climaxes   extinguished
        by moonlight.

sun & moon

your body wraps around mine
like summer heat & I savor
the suffocating humidity
of sweat chilled at twilight.

vinyasa

blood throbs against carotid;
match breath to veins vibrating
soften into
exhalations rolling
               through vertebrae,

grounding into clay
follow   blood
through crown & diaphragm
 e x p a n d s
empty lungs   exhale
lips parting a close
mouthed sigh   diffused
       into   sweet smoke
of   blue sage & juniper

cleansed air as it's sucked
back   into my lungs.

daybreak

a frozen window,
        crystals growing on glass
        vertebrae stacked, and

light streams;
legs twist in linen.
        a leftover braid
        snarls;
nestle closer,
warm as blankets,

curl   into chest.
fingers trace my spine.

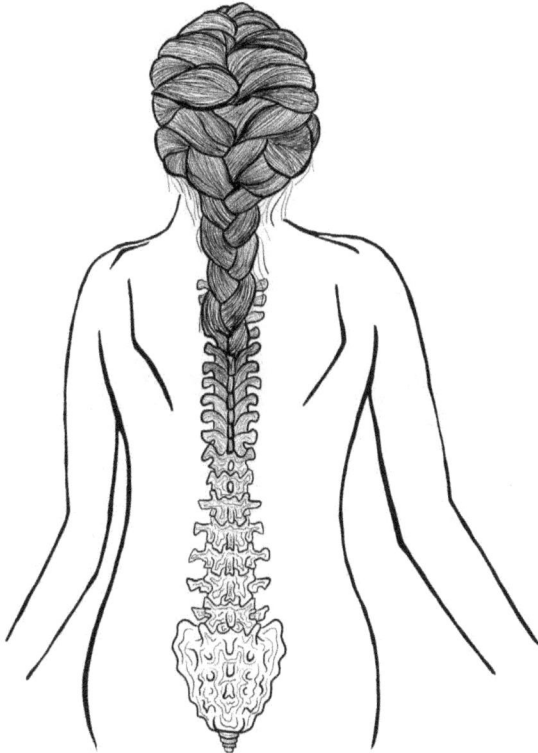

aubade for the sun

I sit in meditation
            shielded by the pier.

sand burns with autumn
                 on the water.

crisp air
sometimes a breeze
brushes   leaves in its wake.

I do my one hundred and eight sun salutations
to welcome   the equinox,
but my heart   is not in it.

**some days,
I live on coffee & acoustic;**

I light the blackened wooden wick,
cracking flame & wax.

the gooseneck kettle shoots
                        boiling water
 around 200 degrees
pour over course,
grounds

sizzling at the bottom
of a stainless steel french press

acoustic guitar
            whispers through speaker
on the other side of the room,

writing with one hand
                & sipping black coffee
                        with the other,

breathe in deep enough,
& I can exhale
                poetry
                like carbon dioxide.

fingerprints & tree rings

flesh still yellow with breath,
concentric growth rings
stained dark sienna.

look closely,
          see the drought & bloom—

I press thumb to center
leaving double loop
among the whorls & wonder

if my fingerprint would linger
to tell my story too.

absence

dark eyes stare through fog
twirl wet hair,   a ring

swathed in the waffle-knit sweater
skin choked with goose bumps
& eyelids fall—

lips painted collarbone indigo
& whispered waves
through vertebrae

the sheets restless
peaks & troughs.

swirl between waves

skin molds to weight,
sunburned heat raises
      ripples to palms
      grazing sacrum.

lips brush jawline
               vertebrae shiver

toes flex   into calves
cementing fingers
to shoulder blades;

      an oyster spat bonds
      to a permanent home;

gasping   for air
      between tides.

anxiety

freezing sweat pools
& skin crawls with sand fleas

aorta swollen with cortisol &   what if
palpitation becomes constant
storm eroding   vessels,
          thinning walls
                    til' fibers snap—

like orbital capillaries
                              bursting
without sleep, because darkness
swallows

& in the abyss
shoulders collapse,
                    consumed
like the hillside shrouded
by marine layer—

wait for the sun
to burn off the fog.

swallowed

drumming waves
match pulse
baring barnacles
as they rear from pilings.

mourning the moon,
pigeons coo nestled
                    in niches;
the pier whines
against break & rip

osprey trills vibrate
            call back
& lose breath to wind.

another shell
consumed by foam.

sunkissed

digging toes into sand course
with oyster shards,
wind cups   jaw
                & kisses—

breathe the ocean as it beats.
the cool sea breeze biting;

cringe &
        grasp at cold hips.

he promised to fill her sky
with light. through dark,
she waits.

on the nights I can't fall asleep

lay in ocean's foam
pulled
      back
          &
      forth
by moon tides and cotton currents
that smell of myrrh
          or is that the tail
          of incense smoke

      stare at the sienna glow

& tree resin
will seal eyelids;
      asphyxiate the nightmares.

anemia

breaths thicken
to the walls of my throat.
everything dimmer—
brown beachgrass, brittle.
the ocean too full of salt,
and feverish laps
on the shoreline.

abandon sand.
I wish I could spread clouds;
poke them with a needle,

like the veins that push
against my skin
full of lethargic blood.

insomnia

crescent sliver shines
luster condensation
trailing window panes
& beat of blades caw—

tangled
waves unified
          breath &
sea salt stings
the other side of the bed
empty

breathe deep
             & slip
          below the surface

mirror

waves smear sketches
churning shells for eyes.

silver or gold gestures
crawl in currents;

my skin marred
           by light
           piercing foam

kept in a glass-cased silhouette;
I break the surface
with one finger.

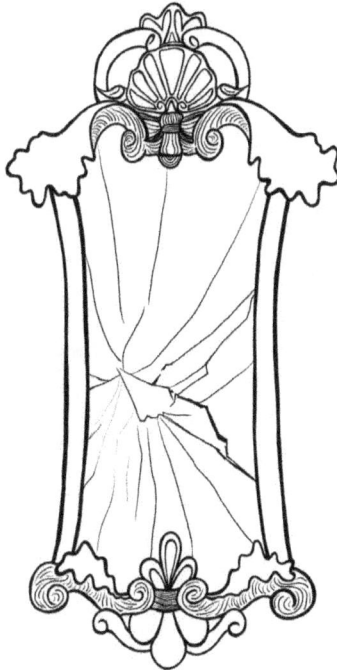

squall

an osprey flies into strobe-lit
cumulus drumming;
leaking humidity
weighs beating wings

buoyant but exposed
sharp light & obsidian
sagging with vapor

clouds charge pulses,
static ripples
pumping rain like blood

and my own veins pulse
to the full moon's tides—
rogue waves spurred
by cobalt canyons &
drowned earthquakes.

nostalgia

draw driftwood close,
smell salt entrenched
flaking grain;
trace a story in splinters,
whispered by barnacles
& sundried algae.

the sandalwood
        branch drowned,
every breath
of bark salt-soaked

abandoned and sucked dry;
peel a piece away
and sacrifice it to fire—

the flame dances
cobalt and lavender
charcoal incensed thyme,
but dioxin plagues,

and just like that,
beauty turns to poison.

neuroma

old trauma
        stuck,

a shard
of oyster shell wedged
between bone
& nerve, tissue

swells
at high tide.

maybe I'll drown.

I fall back into waves
beating against me; pulling hair
spreads and swims,

catches in jellyfish tentacles. minnows
peck my skin until their stomachs gorge

and hold them too far under
the surface. if I swallow salt and sink,

submit to the pull of a rip current, then coral
and anemone might grow on my skull;

my ears ring as the tides
grab handfuls of shells
and steal them away.

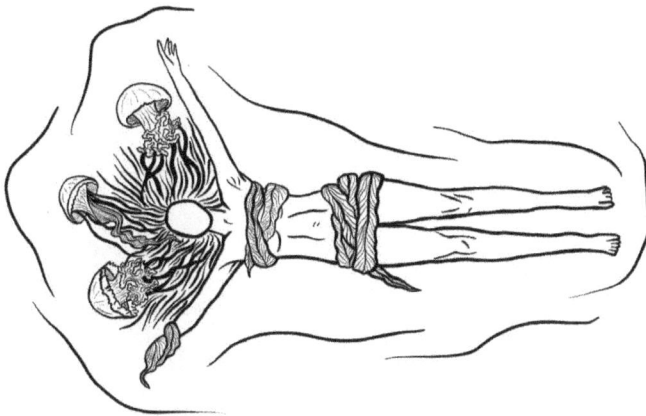

dark syzygy

once a month,
solar & lunar tides collide,
create a void to bathe in.

step forward   vertebrae stacked,

& the shadowed glow
pulls
            everything
                        into
                              alignment.

under pressure

clay balloons in the kiln—
it can crack

riddled with scars
              & stretch marks
no shrinking
can smooth.

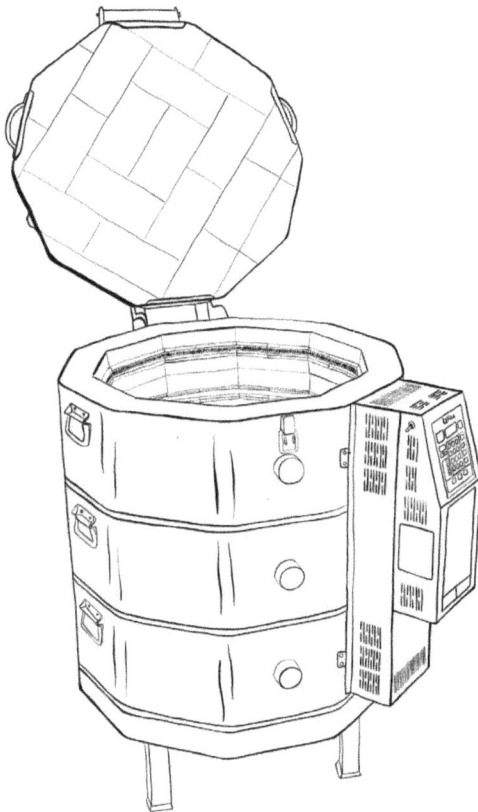

impingement

shells pinch muscle
swollen into edema.
nerves and tendons tangle

in the sinew of seaweed.
tidal strides swell blood,
sucking bone

brittle; ashen driftwood
crumbles between palms,
parched by sea salt. white

shards splinter,
wedge in fingernails
and ligament. bones grind;
I clench my hip.

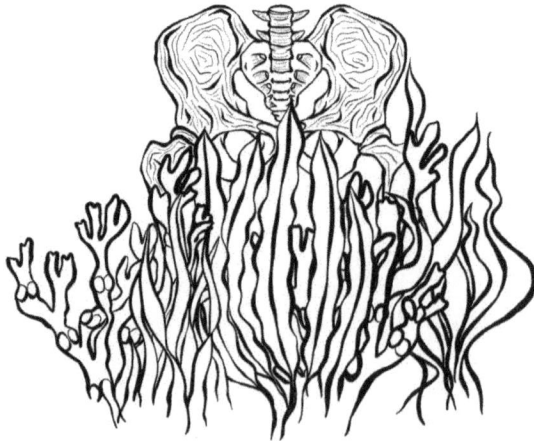

cyclic

synched with the moon
so cycles match;

tides vibrate
with her closeness,
      an empty midnight.

bathe in her shadow

at her fullest, fertile, swollen,
thriving in gentle light seeping
through dusk.

tuning in

trees sway to the beat of breakers:
listen to the pulse that rules the wind,
the hum of our collective sound—

with palms pressed to clay,
I vibrate at the same frequency.

lunar

kyanite, rose quartz, and citrine
                    lined up on the window sill
                    ready to charge with the full moon.
& in the studio carving
craters into clay; waxing & waning
          gibbous surrounding a plump full
cut from slabs, licked & pressed
          to the round body of a mug,
blade stroke gouging flesh.

& as the moon ascends,
          swell the tides,
step into nightfall
baring heart to stars

cradled
where handle meets rim,

so when you press your lips to it,
you can feel the moon rise, too.

illuminated

caught in a rip,
thrashed by waves foaming
at the mouth, biting
skin; dragged
through the sandbar, scratched
against shells, silt
swirling in my hair, I smile
at the moon;
she swaddles me in her light.

blood thins through
translucent skin;

salt courses through veins,
& cleanses me inside out.

pulled further
                    and further

& I almost let the ocean
                    swallow me whole
before the moon
          carries me to shore.

moon bathing

the moon swells;
       sewn to her flesh,
toes buried
          in clay craters.

bathing in starlight   & shadowed sun
             to calm internal waters;
forcing stagnant blood
through estuary veins.

palms open to constellations
as sandalwood burns

my skin vibrates
tidal hum.

arriving

crash into shoreline
alive & grounded
& capable of anything.

becoming

& one day,
her heart cracked—
spread like wildfire,
scorching the dry & dead
tsunami tide rinsing ash

with the clearing,
clarity

blood moon

I refuse to hide my phases,
but to be strong like vinegar,
like the moon pulling ocean
& eclipsing sun.

migration

the male osprey migrates first in summer;
following sun swayed compass,
& the female shadows,
> soaring high on thermals
> traversing desert & sea—

but in winter the female precedes,
guided by moon's wake,
> pausing at the rappahannock
> to catch the spring shad run
& in appalachia
to watch waxing gibbous
rise through blue haze,
> & when she finally returns
> she plunges into shore break
before returning to her nest.

dawn patrol

the moon heaves
waves and chop,
embraced in foam, twirling
against shallows,
submerged
      just long enough
to remind me to breathe.

float to the surface
eyes wide, lungs gasping
      through tangled hair,
the sun swaddles.

growing pains

open your heart to the universe
& let its energy fill you.
open your heart to pain too;

your hurt makes you stronger—

makes you tear down
walls so they can be rebuilt.

ritual

steamed coconut cream caramelizes
darkness; sand dirties
                    crashing waves.

it's hazelnut and honey
not salt,
            that waft
& ginger sips savor
cardamom and cacao

acidity burns taste buds,
then veins;   skin radiates
                    bitter sunburn.

the last drop caressed
by foam;   leftover grounds trail
like sand
            down the walls
of a handmade mug.

molting

press thumb to shoulder.
& the fingerprint lingers.

later, heat leaves
chills & skin prickles
                against sheets

preened flakes slough
to the floor;
            one feather at a time

nails sharp; a beak
picking away at plume

            change happens slow
            like that;

sometimes you don't even notice.

bloom

when the sun enters aries in march
buds begin to blossom, & his heat scalds
earth, scrubs it raw.

laying bare, seared at low tide,
surround sound almost suffocating;
lethargic waves

slough winter skin—
everything touched gleams gold
tanned leather & sun-bleached mane,

wade out, a blooming
lotus floating in salt,
      & rooted in sand.

local

an osprey returns
to nest atop the jetty buoy
reading the ocean & moon
as salt-stained pages.

awake to grey skies
for the homecoming
above the horizon.

wind howls at sand that stings,

wait for the wave that curls
just right; the white cap
hours, synchronized with waning tides.

skydance

cut through cumulus
                    so close to the sun
                    light mirrors composite,
casting glares
on ocean glass,

an osprey in slow
                    undulating avigation
            over the nest
blades scream
            in conversion, and hover
plunging
            feet first,
            props whir
trapping downwash
            swell & surge channel
            back to roost.

golden hour

clouds lined in amber luster;
mirror pink patina
       on sun-bathed sand
& cumulus hovering over glass

it's magic,   air ablaze with
blue-diffused UV basking
      seagrass, shells & skin.

ospreys skydance
to waves crashing shoreline;

& the whole earth sings
           sorcery
as sun and moon
pass incantations.

tangled sheets

grains of sand brushed
from legs
          rubbed together—
they move to rain;
rushing off steel.

gutters reverberate windows;
staccato to breaths   heavy enough
                          to fog mirrors

on skin salted
by rough waves
and pooling sweat.

clouds dry,
          foam churns coast.

adaptation

like an osprey,
I can nest
anywhere;

         but

migration is

         essential.

nesting

wafting scavenged sage
with an osprey feather
brown mottled, charred
at the edge
           where the flame caught

smoke cleansed breath
over abalone & amethyst

settle into the hillside
& serenade the moon
with coyotes' howl.

acknowledgements

first, thanks to everyone at finishing line press for believing in this collection and for turning what felt like a lofty dream, into reality.

thank you to aaron lelito at wild roof journal, for being the first to publish "molting" in issue 8 (my first lit journal publication ever!) and to the editors at seaborne magazine for publishing "insomnia" and "swallowed" in issue 2.

immense gratitude to my whole family, especially my parents, sam and alison bethune, for their steadfast encouragement and support in every dream I chase. to my sister, olivia for always being around to settle my anxiety & for propping me up when I (often) felt like my work wasn't good enough. to bailey, my fellow artist of the fam, for being so enthusiastic about reading my work and offering feedback. and, of course, to all of my grandparents, beryl & sheila anthony, and ed & lana bethune for eagerly supporting all of my pursuits.

to all of the friends that reached out and offered encouragement and enthusiasm along the way, your words & support have meant more than you know. especially you, megan, caitlin, kendra, tarryn, owen, & lauren—for being the best and unconditionally supporting my endeavors, despite how many hundreds of miles separate us. thank you for always making me feel loved, and for being there no matter what.

and to tanner, kacie, and cici—thank all of you so much for helping me take some book promo photos! this has been such an adventure and I can't tell you how much I appreciate y'all taking time to help me out!

I finished writing this book over two years ago now, and have known about it's publication for about a year—in which time I have found a hugely supportive and awesome group of friends out here in california. though I didn't know y'all when I was actually writing the thing, it has meant so much for you all to share the psych with me! especially you, steph & katie, fully do not know what I'd do without you. (also thanks katie for coming in with the assist when I got stuck on the illustration for "becoming".)

a huge thanks to colton zobel for both the gorgeous cover art & for taking my official author photos! it means the world that you let me pair one of your photographs with my first book—I couldn't be more psyched & it truly couldn't be more perfect. I am so grateful for you and our friendship.

shout out to jon pineda, for being an incredible teacher, and for ultimately instilling belief in myself as an author. your feedback & encouragement over the years has been invaluable, and I truly don't know that I would've set out on this endeavor had I not had the benefit of having you as a mentor. I am so appreciative of your support, all the advice and wisdom shared over coffee, and especially that you took the time to write a blurb for my first book!

thank you to katy balma, your kind words & realness mean more than you know. to kelli agodon for your support, enthusiasm & stunning recommendation. I couldn't have dreamt of more heartening reviews of my work.

and to brandon—without you, this collection wouldn't have a love story. thanks for giving me one worth writing about, and for your love & support as I chase my dreams. I am incredibly grateful for you.

and of course, to you, reader, for supporting my art and reading this compilation of words, memories and dreams. it's a scary thing to put out into the world, but I am so happy this book found it's way to you.

nicole bethune winters is a poet, writer, ceramic artist, & yoga teacher. by day, (& often night) she makes and sells pottery in her home studio, which she built herself shortly after moving to california. she is also studying to become a yoga therapist.

nicole began writing *brackish,* her debut collection, in a poetry seminar while studying creative writing at the university of mary washington, and continued documenting her life through these poems as she moved across the country. her writings are inspired by her connection to and exploration of nature, as well as her artistic processes. her poetry has been published in wild roof journal, backlash journal and seaborne magazine.

when she isn't writing or wheel-throwing, nicole is likely at the beach, on a trail, or exploring new landscapes. she derives most of the inspiration for her creative work from her interactions with the environment around her, and is always looking for new ways to connect with and understand the earth.